To Dearest Debra

Grace to the World

D1246626

Searching

JAN SCHOMP

BALBOA.
PRESS
A DIVISION OF HAY HOUSE

Balboa Press books may be ordered through booksellers or by contacting:

Balboa Press
A Division of Hay House
1663 Liberty Drive
Bloomington, IN 47403
www.balboapress.com
1 (877) 407-4847

Because of the dynamic nature of the Internet, any web addresses or links contained in this book may have changed since publication and may no longer be valid. The views expressed in this work are solely those of the author and do not necessarily reflect the views of the publisher, and the publisher hereby disclaims any responsibility for them.

The author of this book does not dispense medical advice or prescribe the use of any technique as a form of treatment for physical, emotional, or medical problems without the advice of a physician, either directly or indirectly. The intent of the author is only to offer information of a general nature to help you in your quest for emotional and spiritual well-being. In the event you use any of the information in this book for yourself, which is your constitutional right, the author and the publisher assume no responsibility for your actions.

Print information available on the last page.

ISBN: 978-1-5043-3383-2 (sc)
ISBN: 978-1-5043-3384-9 (hc)
ISBN: 978-1-5043-3382-5 (e)

Library of Congress Control Number: 2015908711

Balboa Press rev. date: 9/8/2015

Table of Contents

3
<u>Searching In Chaos</u>

4
<u>Searching In Life</u>

5
<u>Searching In Memories</u>

6
<u>Searching Sideways</u>

7
<u>Searching Ended – Beginning</u>

Dedication

To my children, who gave to me so much life!

From the first moment I heard your heartbeat
Through the monitor
I knew, I knew,
God had heard this beating first
In your heart even before time.
In all God's magnificent planning and creating
God attached your heart to mine.

From the first moment that I heard you cry,
I knew God's milk began to flow.
In response to you in this natural way
That only Mother Gods can know.

I knew God had heard
Your own special sound,
The songs you would someday sing.
Like sweet morning birds
Gently awakening with love.

When I saw your eyes
I knew your soul,
For those eyes spoke to me of the God
Who made eyes, the power to see
All that God imagined first!
Those eyes could also see
The dream within my heart.
Filled with fulfillment and becoming
Of both you and I.

As I drew you to my center, to suckle life,
The mystery of milk and love,
I smelled you as I held you in my arms,
And I knew God had delighted in smelling you first.
For your essence was alluring
Like that of gods and goddesses.
Among whom you would also now take your place.

Ah....but when I touched you,
That is when I knew God had touched you first,
For you had earthly _life_ within you. You were alive,
And you were here with me.
Finally...as it was always meant to be.
For in some other world
I had chosen you, and you had chosen me.
And it was more than my imagination could take in!
Dreaming, planning, hoping, yearning, trusting
All together hand and hand.
Joyfully dancing, gracefully circling
Our moment of bonding.
Our moment of love
This first grand waltz of our belonging.

And this was the time that
Mother God joined with me,
In adoration, yes adoration
Of the promise of you.
And in this one moment
Outside of time, is captured forever
In a heavenly album of love.
An image of
You to me, me to you, God to life,
As I welcomed you into my arms and heart.
Each and every one of you!
My dearest precious children of love.

Foreword

Too many women writers have not been able to publish their writing. While it is a shame, it is not surprising that history has made it more difficult for women's voices to be recorded than men's. When I was a child, my father's status as a writer was made clear to me and my siblings by the space that surrounded him while he worked at his desk or in his armchair; it was a sacred space that demanded distance and silence from us. He spent much of his time in that space. The time my father spent writing, reading, and thinking was off-limits to us, a rule I remember being enforced not only by him but by my mother, who supported and protected his status. I grew up with a healthy respect not only for his work but for the vocation of writers in general, a vocation that seemed at the time to be entirely separate from my, my sisters', and my mother's habits of note-taking in letters, journals, stories, and essays.

I am a writer, perhaps in some ways like my father, but more significantly, I am a writer like my mother. My mother's writing space was harder for me and my siblings to recognize as children, but it was always there in the words she whispered into our ears, the stories she told us at bedtime, the books she put into our hands. It was there not in a distant way that encouraged reflection and awe but rather in the consecrated crevasses of everyday contact, in the intimate touches of a mother who discovered the power of her own voice through relationships with others and with God. In my life, my mother's presence has been like the voice of Mother God, who says to her child, "I wean you / To tell your own life story; / Therein lies a mother's glory." On my best days, I am like my mother and also undeniably myself, able to embrace the particular sanctities of my own life as she does of hers in her poetry.

In the past few years of retirement and reflection, my mother has claimed her own sacred armchair zone, a mental and spiritual space where, as she says, "I speak of my quest for peace. / I think of questions too delicate to speak / Out loud. I whimper and swallow / Words as well as tea." I continually search for and find her in this space that requires neither distance nor silence but rather is as open and connected as her arms are to her grandchildren.

Through her work to make this book, my mother has taught me again how to "be conscious / And wake up!"—how to search for what matters most and how to do the work to be true to it. It is a gift she offers to all of her readers. It is a "novena," certainly—each poem like a worn and polished bead threaded together in a rosary of searching that finds its home in the very act of continual reaching.

Claire Schomp

SEARCHING

Beyond

Beyond our seeing,
Hearing, smelling,
Tasting and touching;
Beyond our word,
Thought, and choosing:
Beyond our imagining,
Dreaming and doing...

Beyond our dancing,
Frolic, family, work and play
And our own special way.
Beyond our creating,
Love and hating;
Beyond living and dying each day...

Beyond our art,
Our poetry and storytelling;
Beyond our rituals,
Devotion and prayer.
Beyond consciousness,
Transcendent meditations,
Which take us elsewhere...

Beyond, beyond, beyond
Somewhere, everywhere,
Yet beyond
In the void of that empty place
So singularly rare.
Passionately
Incomprehensibly
Intimately
Within
I will meet you there!

Oh My God (OMG)

I am weary of searching for you, my God;
My longing is my energy's worst enemy.
I have prayed and danced.
I have been reverent and cynical
Like a devil with a halo.

I have had tidal waves of enlightenment,
Pitch black dark nights of the soul,
And days of harmony and days of boredom.
I am tired of hide and seek.

Merciful grace has been poured into
The beautiful basin of my soul,
Miraculously spilling over the top
While holes in the bottom are always emptying, emptying!

I have seen us on the mountaintop,
Oh the magnificence of Thee.
With time however I collapse into
Forgetting all that we could be.

I give up I will say no more; I will listen not!
I am like the still rubber ball forgotten by children,
Growing mold upon my surface
And lying in the deep damp green grass.

Oh My God!
I am in the air again...
Flying!

God Let Go

God let go.
Rupturing, exploding
From God's own light.
Stars twinkled
In the dark of night.
Bluest blue filled
The endless ocean,
The boundless horizon.
God let go
Of the burning sun:
Yellows and reds,
Unfathomable light
Shattered into rainbows,
Warmth and delight.
From God's wholeness
In furious flight,
God created
Discerning light.

God let go
From silence to sound.
Waves pounded,
Thunder rolled
Lightning cracked,
Children laughed
Birds chirped and
People cried.
Lions roared,
Rockets soared,
Water leaked
And mice squeaked.

And that still quiet
Inner voice
Broke
The sound barrier
Of our soul.

God let go
From stillness
Birthing
Moving, living, growing,
Ever changing anew.
Seeds sprouted eagerly
Out of the ground.
Insect and animal
Human being abound.
And, in the letting go,
Creating all we
Have come to know.

God let go.
Of forgiveness.
Betrayals of our freedom.
Transforming our choices
Evil or good.
Restoring us always
To forgotten nobility,
Inalienable beauty.
God let go
Of Mercy and
Love!

Nursing Mother God

The Child:
Do not wean me
Mother God
From your tender breast,
Let me suckle
Till the end
Of my day.
Let me be dependent
In an obvious way.
Spare me
Doubt,
Risk,
Daring,
And giving.
In other words
Spare me living!
Be present and warm
And close and safe.
Please
Do not wean me
From your tender breast.

Mother God:
Dear Child
Be conscious
And wake up!
Do not nod off;
Rise up and be!
You are not me.
I set you down
Upon your feet

To walk free!
Move quickly,
Go forward,
Respond,
Live life,
Experience you, and create.

I let you go
To be – to grow.
I wean you
To tell your own life story;
Therein lies a mother's glory.

Life –
Touch it,
Savor it,
Enter into it and expand.
Doubt and dare;
Risk and challenge.
Be bold,
Give and lose,
Love and hate.
Rather I free you
To give generously of
Your own milk of life and love,
To be, all that We can be.

Tiny Words of Love

Tiny toddler girl
Rises from her slumber.
The early morning light
Pierces through the edges
Of her window shades.
She gathers her teddy,
Her blankie, her pacifier.
She toddles to the hallway window,
Her head held high in hope.
Her large brown eyes scan
The cars below to see
If her mama has gone to work
For this day.

Her curly topped head
Drops in resignation.
Disappointed in her tiny heart,
She moves slowly
To find another
Who can never equal her.
She for whom she longs,
To fill her day with love.
The little girl's living and loving
Is redirected
By someone else for another day.
"Mama mama" she whispers,
Her tiny, tiny words of love.

God of Light
Illuminating gradually
With gentle

Ultimate innocence.
You call it the dawn.
You sit in anticipation
Of some small utterance:
A tiny word of gratitude
For a still beating heart,
Food for breakfast,
A secret to hold in confidence,
The sun that brightens,
The rain that quenches
The thirst of the earth.
Like your thirst, Oh God
For words spoken to You,
Your love is so vast,
So deep, so complete.

You listen hopefully,
Scanning, ever scanning,
Waiting, ever waiting,
Longing, ever longing,
For a moment of newly created dawn.
To fill empty moments, mute stillness
With little recognition,
Caring or attention.
Your lonely outpouring of Love.
Your longing will never be
Redirected or pacified.
You wait eternally, patiently
For *tiny, tiny* words of love.

Come With Me

Using silence as the mode of my transportation,
I have traveled to that boundless place.
Past the soft sensual sand beneath my feet,
Past the song of ocean wave in my ear,
Beyond the color and perfume of flowers-
Delicate, fragile, fragrant blooms of my garden.
Away from the mountain's clear and fresh air
Cleansed by trees of elegant standing.
Children delighting in butterflies
Past happy times of simple fun.
Dancing in shadows cast by the sun
Away from brilliant inspiration,
Understandings and moments of care.
Beyond opening up and becoming aware.

Oh come with me – come with me
And pull me back when I long to stay.
This still and silent place of mysterious love
For which I would give life's breath away.

Imagery Meditation

Deep in meditation,
I am witnessing Jesus transfigured on the mountaintop,
And His clothes become dazzling white.
My desire heightens to transfigure along with Him.
I respond; my yearning creates movement
With electrifying speed.
This is my Beloved.
Listen to (her)!
I experience being one, the one, the Beloved!
I drink in the dazzling light.
Conscious enlightenment!
I feel such joy, such consolation,
And then – I remember, or do I forget?
Sweet life in time,
Sweet heartbeat of mine.
In between I speak: "Draw me ever forward to You
Oh divine light and love."

I hold firm: I stop: I resist,
I seem not ready, yet I am lured on.
My soul aware, he is consuming me
Divine union, moment divine.
My timelessness away from time.
I choose to return to
Forgetfulness and fear.
Am I not yet awake?
Ah! Yet I will cherish the memory,
And someday I will give up the treasures of here
For the treasures of there.
Or are they the same?
For I am here
When I am there!

The One Breath of God

There is but one breath,
The eternal breath of God.
It resides in that still space
That lies between
Your breath in and your breath out.
It is like dead air caught between two windows.
That moment before
A moan of ecstasy.
The welling up from the deep earth
Before wailing begins.
It is the eye of the hurricane,
Tranquil, static, exciting, threatening, challenging.
It is the seventh wave,
A space which might present someone
With a chance?
To make something different:
An intention to create,
A change,
An outcome of goodness.
This breath comes not from the lungs
But from the heart.
A heart, that chooses to breathe
In harmony with
The one breath of God!

Where Are You God

Where are you God,
Untouchable, unseen Mystery?
I look for the sun,
But it is night.
I see windows filled with steam
That keep the clouds from sight.
Oil and tree roots
That I know are there,
Buried deep under, somewhere.
You are there, yet where, oh where?

Where are you God
Who eludes me so?
If I were to cut out my spirit
I would surely die.
That spirit which I know and feel is there.
Filled with intense longing
Unrelenting, restless
Wanting and yearning
Always for you.
Oh so curious, so mysterious
This be-longing to You!
This oh so visible
Brilliantly resplendent
Union of love, I have with you.

SEARCHING IN NATURE

Tree of Life

It is not because I have lost faith in your teachings
Or have abandoned the openness and ardor of my youth.
I was but a root with one small branch blowing in the wind.
I acknowledged that you were my source and I would survive
Both the rodent called the devil and the occasional rage of
storms.
I was dependent on you and turned to you for
Every moment of suffering and grief I endured.
I begged you for release and relief,
And you poured upon me sunshine
Along with the rain. With the leaves of my past
I was nourished and encouraged and supported.
One day the elements no longer seemed to affect me.
It was as though I was not like a tree;
I was a tree! The tree of You and me.
Finally standing so tall, seemingly reaching to the sky
I began to see as You saw,
And all around me was such lavish and beautiful abundance!
My beliefs I shed like my leaves in the fall.
For they were based upon my vulnerability
And fears of being small. Now the power within my
Branches, fastens and holds
The ripening of my fruit,
The deliciousness of gratitude,
The widening of my understanding,
The inclusiveness of my view,
The knowing of my purpose,
The blessing of knowing You
In all the stages of my becoming.
You were raising me up
To recognize, that the rings within me

Were always You. I was your purpose,
My purpose was You!
You invite me now come
Come as one to celebrate the harvest!

Love in Vermont

In the stillness
Of the pitch dark night
I approach,
Sleepy and vulnerable,
To experience
This silent beauty
Of glimmering snowflakes
Gracefully
Free falling.

I feel youthful passion
Awakened from frozen time.
Intense and tender ardor
Satisfy and warm my soul.
Ah, beautiful wonder,
In your nocturnal silence
You humble me.
I reverence thee
Breathlessly!

From the swelling of my heart
I speak in deepest adoration.
How I love you, deepest shimmering mystery.
As the snow caresses me,
Gently tasting and touching my lips,
Within the serene, stark stillness I hear
"I love you too."

Choice

I sit and stare
At the crusted snow.
Sunshine glares;
Making ice caps aglow.

I long to make footprints
That shift and crack open
New possibilities
In this vision.

Ah, but it is dangerous,
Ever such a slippery step.
What if I fall before I even begin?
Will I step out again?
Is the shift too bold, the crack too new?
Is the design uncertain?
Will its possible change
Be as grand as before?

Yet if I go and lead the way,
Others might follow,
Making new their own design
And generating new possibilities.

All that was
Will be as new.
I create with awareness
Of everything I can do.

I gaze carefully
Within my soul.
As I always do, whenever I feel
Aglow with choice!

Falling Leaves

The year is beginning to come to an end
I ponder memories, as I walk in the glen.
Dipping temperatures, a shivering look
To review memories in my open book.

Pages of feelings about past events,
Kicking leaves, jolting where energy was spent.
Emotional sensitivity I wish to fall away
Those hearty green leaves of yesterday.

I soul search things I feel guilty for
On a carpet of crackling crispy floor.
These stories and thoughts I have carefully weaved
I now notice it is what I have come to believe.

I have carried them around like this big heavy tree
And now that I look they are painful for me.
If I truly wish to be all I can be
I must shed deadly beliefs, like these falling leaves.

The Source

Imagine me as a bottomless hidden lake
Embedded in the highest heavenly mountain top.
Misty, shadowy clouds forming around,
Longing to embrace me.

I collect every raindrop
And snowflake which falls into my azure blue.
I trickle outward,
Here, there,
Endlessly, generously
Giving bountiful water
For life.

To strolling streams and
Bubbling brooks,
Rolling rivers and, lazy lakes,
Water-holes and waterfalls,
Marshes and wetlands,
Prairies and wastelands,
Forest and woodlands,
Farmlands and orchards,
Fields and gardens, every wet and dry surface.
Reservoirs, recesses formed in the ground,
Of this mighty thirst quenching earth.

Every single moment
Of every single day,
I flow.
To big, open cupped hands
And pitchers, cups and basins carried on one's head.
To bottles, bowls and barrels.

Leather skins and bird baths
For feathered wings.
Oh the joy I give
Watering living things.

There is only one thirst to quench:
The longing and yearning of
Every living being-
Earth's family bonded by creation-
Related through
This unifying simple basic need.
This swishing drain of my compassionate
Equalizing necessity,
A symbol for all to see, with every knowing eye!

Go now, gather all creatures of the earth,
And all pieces and particles
Joined and fixed by this force,
For this vital essential water of life!

Blow the trumpets,
Sound the tambourine.
Gather all to give pristine gratitude!
Expose and espouse this enlightenment
That all IS one!
Hold high the sacred basin.
Have all sing and dance
To the rhythm of the falling rain.
This splashing, soaking, drenching music of life.
Welcome all to the table Mother Nature has set,
For this, this water is ME!
I am the Source; I am this wet and wonderful stuff of life!

The Secret

I speak:
Oh lovely flower,
Exquisite mystery
Singularly stunning
Please whisper a secret to me.
The flower speaks:
I was a tiny seed
Planted in rich dark desire.
Our ritual dance in springtime
That lights a heart afire.
Connecting with deep grounded need,
I lie in earthly bedding for a seed to aspire.
Lovers longing only to feed
What nature is designed to heed.

When you decided to create,
I let go; I chose my fate.
Embedded in this nesting place,
Lovers in a passionate embrace.
I became engaged in a cosmic race,
A climax only described as grace!
Thriving, growing without asking why,
Breaking my shell with an enormous sigh,
I stretched joyfully toward the sky.
Beginning to sprout, beginning to grow
Strengthening, dreaming, and getting to know.
How nurturing can bring to a glow
The joy of letting it all go slow.
Nature is constant; abundance will flow.

Back and forth of caring and giving,
Sometimes failing, then forgiving
Discoveries of truly living.
Nothing seems to be forbidden;
Patterns revealed, some still hidden!

Growing often thrives on a little teasing;
Progress only thwarted through self-treason.
Feeling longing for no other reason,
Passionately responding, never ceasing,
Budding and blossoming in the proper season.

I will exist in time, and you will see
That which I am meant to be,
And if you speak clearly what it is you see
You will give witness to the glory of me.
Treat me gently; take care of me.
Beauty is our shared destiny
Forever in God's memory.

To Be

Has the soil refused the seedling in the spring?
Have the insects gone on strike about things?
Or the birds quit and no longer sing?
Have animals quit doing their thing?

Only humans question what to do
Or argue about how it should be.
Imagining other ways to see,
And making mistakes to be ever more free.

Like the soil and the seedling,
The song of the birds,
Our joy is in living
Where we are meant, to simply be!

Bird Talk

In the still quiet of that time
Between dawn and sunrise
As dim light peeks in the corner
Of my slightly open eyes,
When I begin to think of You
I hear the birds
Stirring from their nestled sleep.
Chirping eloquently, each little peep.
Arousing to nature and the new day,
My morning worship fades away.

Profoundly curious to know what
These birds are saying,
I realize, this, this is praying!
Do they give praise and glory to You?
Do they ask you what it is You do?
Do they give gratitude for another day?
Do they speak of things I long to know?
Why is it languages are coded so?
Are birds really free in all their simplicity?
To reveal in chirps of glee
An early morning litany
Of love and worship to Mystery!

The Flexible Tree

Life for me is like a tree on a journey,
A journey of growing up, straight toward the heavens!
My life is ever present, or so it seems,
For I stand resolutely in my ground.
I observe; I listen;
I feel what presses against me.
I hold my opinions and my beliefs
Rigidly with purity.
Yet with each new season
I experience the birth and the death
Of ideas as numerous as lush green leaves.
So I have learned
When to loosen up, relax, stretch and bend.
In response to life's wind and snow
To recognize it is not about
What I am sure that I know.
Depending on my uncertainty
Or perhaps my respectability,
This moment of unpredictability
Calls me to *bend*
With necessary flexibility!

Love Leaves

Floating leaves on an autumn day-
Splendid sparkling array
Twirling in a gentle breeze-
Would you like to dance with me?
Butterflies and birds flutter
Passionately in the air.
Affectionate foliage touches me everywhere.
I breathe in the fine fragrance of Thee.
Lying down in a bed of grass,
A bed dressed in harvest hue,
I open my arms to your caress
From every surrounding tree.
Breeze, sunshine and
Gentle falling leaves.
Oh lovely awesome Mystery.
You bring all together in harmony
Simply to make love to me!

Little Spider

Little spider, little mite
Crawling on me in the night.
I switch on my bed- lamp light,
To squish you before you bite.
As you push on to avoid the fight,
I ask myself, is squishing right?

You seem to want to crawl and soar
Life emerges from your tiny core.
My sleep is now in an uproar,
So off you go gently to the floor.
Life is a gift and so much more;
I made it through the moral door!

SEARCHING
IN CHAOS

Culture

Please sweetheart
Do not pull at that.
That is your skin!
She looked lovingly at her,
So tiny and thin.

Your skin she said
Your skin, your skin!
She thought for a moment.
It's what you are in!
Oh the mystery of life
What a wonderful thing.

A new little word
For my child of two.
Skin! She laughed again,
Skin is all over you.
But then in an instant
Her laugh turned to a frown.
Dear God,
Take care of this child
Inside, outside
And all around. The mystery of life
Is so profound.

For inside that skin
Is my precious one.
More precious than anything
Under the sun.
Nothing but nothing
Is more precious within

Than my small child
Wrapped in soft skin.
The mystery of life
Is a wonderful thing.

Isn't it strange she thought?
Skin is something
I don't think much about.
Except when I notice
Something about it
That is good or bad.
Only then is when I feel it
Inside and out.
Oh the mystery of life
What is it about?

Living in a culture
Is like skin on me.
It is often something
I don't even see,
Or understand
That it is a certain way.
I just live inside it
Every day.

Like symbols I am told
That represent me.
Chevrolet and apple pie
Or a cherry tree.
Football and baseball
Or even Thanksgiving Day.
Must I organize myself
In this American way?
What is this mystery of living
In a cultural way?

Children in daycare
Men and women full of stress.
Divorce and abortion
Drugs and homelessness.
It is even acceptable to
Look the other way.
In my culture it is just
Part of my day.
This mystery of living
God! What can I say?

I wait in lines,
In traffic too.
I get angry at people
For certain things
That they do.
I watch politicians
On the T.V.
Without even thinking
They reflect me!
I behave always with
An American face.
For I would not
Do some of these things
In some other place.
This mystery of division
In the human race.

Together we do things
To one another
In a style that shows our ways.
Like gesturing and mannering
Throughout our days.
We don't even notice

The person we are.
We need to stop
Think, reflect and care.
Become aware!
Of the power we are in.
For it is not as strong
As what is
<u>Inside of our skin!</u>

Within a culture
Is each precious one.
More precious than anything
Under the sun.
Nothing but nothing
Reflects God
In reality
The same as you
Or the same as me.

Wake up
Pay attention
To what we can do.
We are placed on this earth
To creatively renew.
The skin of the earth
Is waiting for you!

Notice it, touch it
Love it actively.
Think always of creative
Things you can do.
Transform your culture
Do what you can
Until the word "precious"

Is used for every woman and man.
Oh the mystery of life
So profound.
Inside and outside, and all around.

Gangs of the World

I was born into a gang, catholic I mean.
I was faithful and always devout
Though sometimes disturbed by feelings of doubt.

The gang judged acts of immorality.
God was on our side; our leader was right.
Too bad for other gangs who lacked such insight.

Gangs are all separate, divided by fear
Willing to die for faith and fame.
Though the cost will ultimately be,
A history of shame.

Gangs have medals, statues and such,
Stories, rituals and special feast days.
Strangely alike in so many ways.

Gangs are willing to rumble and kill,
Surging often like a violent tide.
While collective consciousness scurries to hide.

We hurt and kill those aspects of others
Differences we declare as oddly apart.
As though it does not affect the health of our very own heart.

We seek to expose and condemn others
Instead of gazing at our own crippling fears.
Gangs! Let us gather at the altar of mirrors.

Gather and proclaim the love in our stories
Choose the most radical and reckless dare.
Sit, just sit with everyone, everywhere.

Sit in the stillness and become aware
Nothing can ever be won.
The human race, the planet, the universe,
Everything is ONE.

Dust

I walk along the shore,
Breezes failing to refresh my breath.
I am choking on dust.
A Good Friday of anguish and death.

This earthquake,
This energy below my feet.
Impermanence concretely observed,
Universal wisdom in the street.

Dust, dust, everywhere dust,
Everything and everyone who has piled up and rotted away.
In this place, in this space,
Now is simple dust, blowing in this day.

I wipe away its heaviness
And weep for its messiness
Until I scoop it into my hand.
In this instant *dust* becomes uniquely grand.

My fingers feel a tiny girl,
A beautiful blossom, a giant tree.
A gallant soldier killed in battle,
A mighty fortress for all to see.

This little boy from cave dwelling days
Who laughed and cried as he played.
A mighty rock where lovers gathered,
A lost sheep from his herd had strayed.

Dust, dust, everywhere dust,
My tears fall gently upon thee.
Earthquakes rearranging eternally.
Will you someday help someone remember me?

Haiti

Earth heaving devastation
Crushing, exploding
Thrusting structures
Falling on top of themselves.
Hitting, missing, breaking,
Killing, wounding or by chance
Eluding thereof.

Human terror.
Anguish erupting
Into screams of horror!
Hand covered heads,
Fruitless defense
To flying, crushing
Steel and cement.
Or witnessing by chance
The frightening, furious
Futility thereof.

Response outpouring.
Chaotic prayerful
Cries for mercy.
Tears of horror.
Paralyzing disbelief.
Tormenting powerlessness.
Gripping uselessness.
Images transfixing human consciousness.
Gratitude for being spared.
Weeping for common humanity
No chance of evading thereof.

In every place,
Crushed, dead and buried alive.
Trapped or terrified
Dry and airless,
Coma or clawing,
Enclosed and entombed.
Resigned or screaming with hope.
Everywhere and no-where
Within disaster, response or even the lack thereof.
Ever present
Is God
Wailing with her children.

The Crucifixion of Japan

Oh Japan
Your foundation convulsed,
Capturing you,
Betraying you,
Scourging your ordinary day.
Imprisoning you in dark places
No human place to stay.
Your courage whipped and beaten,
Exposed to the world.
And mortified, still
You affirm your identity.
Oh Japan, oh misery!

Sentenced again...
To a tsunami
Sweeping tears rearranging
Destruction, anguish and chaos.
Scourged and devastated
You look upon your former
Familiar places and faces.
They are all swept away
Swept away out to sea.
Oh Japan, oh misery.

Heart wrenching, humbling
The disrobing, the destruction
Of your sustaining power.
The explosion like mockery
In your darkest hour.
Fire and poison fill the air;
You acknowledge to the world

Its hopeless pathetic glare.
Standing there for all the world to see
Oh Japan, oh misery.

Oh Japan. Oh Japan.
Lay down and be nailed.
To a cross that has stripped you of life.
Your people gone
Washed out to sea.
Those who are left
Forever damaged
Psychologically.
Oh Japan, oh misery.

Beneath your cross
A three-fold sword
Piercing your being.
Your last drop of blood,
Your last drop of water,
Washes out to the sea.
Contaminated, abandoned,
You hang for all to see.
Oh Japan, oh misery.

We wail;
We cry to the heavens,
From the abyss of mother earth,
Who holds you in her arms.
Her pleas are so profound
Sobbing with alarm.
How long will you be in the tomb?

Oh Japan, oh misery
Within the rubble
Of hearts broken
Lie seeds of desire and hope.
Generosity and love
Planted in mankind
Forever germinating
Resurrection and recovery!

SEARCHING
IN LIFE

Change

Ignorance around change
Is a drape of disregard.
The notions one clings to, like
Some things never change
I will never change
I am still the same person I was
There are absolutes
God never changes...
Create an oblivious attire
That appears before the wise who know you
As rags you have designed
From the old patterns you repeatedly use.

From the moment of the beginning
Of everything everywhere,
Of you, of the first moment of your adornment,
Every moment to follow
Will experience change!
Change, so there it is,
A fine hat to put upon your head.

The great deceiver is not the horned devil,
The dark shadow, or ghost in your mind,
But the lie! The mind that constructs "beliefs,"
"Beliefs" that become false gods!
That is why the first commandment is so powerful and put first.
False gods are always playing dress-up with lies,
Theories, facts and easy excuses!
Especially Grand about Ourselves!

Children playing dress-up
In their enthusiasm for the game of life
Throw off one costume for another
And start the game all over again!
Start over again! Start over again,
For this is the way of God.
We are the embodiment of the
Ongoing, ever-changing eternal God!
Christians say "Put on Christ!"
Who they say made the ultimate change.

Change is a gift called process
Beautifully endowed, gilded in all that is.
Look upon your present beliefs
Especially about yourself,
For until you do, the costumes of your life
Will never be a good fit for you.
To dress in the reality of change is
To see grace right there in the mirror.
As you embody an aura of transformation
In which you fully address the present
To the ever-changing present moment!

Who Am I

It is OK for me to NOT know who I am.
I have been searching for that four leaf clover
For as long as I can remember.
Understanding myself is like naming
All the stars in the sky –
So vast and so far away.
Yet with each step closer
I *change* and become farther away!
Is it because I love myself so much that I pursue who I AM?
Or am I just as much a curious monkey as everyone else
seems to be
About this eternal question?
Believing the search will never end
Yet knowing
That I know and have always known
Who I Am completely
As I marvel in the creation of me!
When I look back,
I see all I have become,
And it excites and awakens me
To continue on
To become all that I can be!

Yet there are those times
I greatly fear
That I am not enough.
That I am poor or not smart enough
Or in so many ways, not quite right.
And my lifelong foreboding
Of not being enough
Is one big cover-up

A smoke screen, a self-inflicted sabotage
For not remembering and remaining in that state.
That state where I look in the mirror of my soul
And see what *is* and fully accept
My perfect creation,
My own I Am!

Fire and Glory

I sit staring at a dancing fire,
Transfixed on flames consuming a log.
Like a grave, likewise being stared at
As it consumes forever the body of a woman.
The heat warms my chilled bones,
Like her smiles, hugs and steaming hot food.
Was she tall and sprightly like these flames
Always kind of dancing as she burned her years?
Did she know she was born to give fruit, shelter,
Warmth, light, harvest?
Like this tree that burns,
Still giving
Generously and gloriously!

Joy

He rode upon a donkey,
Gathering followers and friends.
She shuffled from the kitchen stove
To the table and back again.

He climbed the stairs to an upper room,
Family and friends joining him.
She called to all her family,
Waving and gathering them in.

They gazed upon him as he took the bread;
They watched him as he bowed his head.
She waited till they all sat down;
She led a prayer, and there was no sound.

He blessed the bread and broke it up;
He took the wine and filled the cup.
She ladled into plates the warm and tasty food;
She cut the loaf and set a happy mood.

He shared himself for them to see
And simply said "Remember Me."
She delighted when they cleaned their bowl;
She watched them, and it filled her soul.

For both it was a simple meal,
Memories of love made reverently real.
Memories in one's heart, not just in one's head,
Of love wrapped up in wine and milk and bread.

We try to make such stories
Better or "other" or just not the same.
Yet He would be the first to say
Sharing is love; *joy* is its name.

Asking Nothing In Return

Father Sun rises each morning,
Faithfully arousing Mother Earth
To daylight and daytime movement.
Not that she sleeps!
Her waterfalls pour out, her oceans wave,
Emotions like currents emerge –
Heart-rending, surging, or softly rolling.
Her winds blow; her rains fall
Knocking things down, making things swell.
Her snow lavishes cold climes;
Closed hearts stay frozen in time.
Her warm places grow plants
Even in the dark of night,
And her people seek love
In energetic lovemaking,
Responding to hot deep desires
For growing and deepening love.

Her trains run over old yet well-laid tracks,
Minds ruminating over otherness.
Her planes keep flying
Like ideas that can reach the sky!
Her cars keep driving,
And some of her people keep walking
To get nowhere, to places that have been labeled somewhere.
Wars rage on, battlefields everywhere
Including phony so-called sacred places.
Peacemakers wake up with new ideas
To heal the earth

Contemplatives pray all the night long.
And evil commences business as usual.

Eons of giving and giving,
And still these parents of unconditional love
Ask nothing in return.

Morning Ritual of Praise

Incense rising from my morning cup of tea,
I sip the Eucharist of gratitude for the coming day.
Cup in hand like a hymnal, stirring me,
I go within to listen to your homily.

Silently you speak, inviting me.
So secret, so intimate, I listen.
You speak of my world...my so-called
Problems, insecurities, fears, my sins.

I sip, steam rising...a sacrifice?
A novena, a devotion,
A ritual of days gone by.
Life, a religious constant motion!

Bible stories long put aside,
Saints and songs compromised.
Voices quieted inside of me
Yet prayers alive and memorized.

I speak of my quest for peace.
I think of questions too delicate to speak
Out loud. I whimper and swallow
Words as well as tea.

I begin to think about my day;
Like the steam from my tea, I float away.
Nourished and up and ready to go,
Amazed at how you love me so!

Precious

I am so loved by You;
Your gracious blessings excessive
Have made me feel precious.
Diamonds and pearls, rubies and sapphires
Delicate blossoms, beauty so fair,
Unusual species, all things rare,
Always subject to the utmost care.

I have been nurtured and cherished
Always in your empowering radiant stare.
While seeing myself as weak and fair.
Yet with your boundless love
I have begun to feel rare,
My worth rising high into the air.
To see my own preciousness there.

Oh if I could love
All whom I find so rare in my heart,
Who find their belonging in me
As I find mine in you.
Then I would love them specially
In an utterly perfect way.
I would be "the love of God";
I would love them preciously.

Heaven

My grandson asked me about heaven
At six years of age.
He asked about this final play
On life's unfolding stage.

His eager eyes begged lovingly
For me to describe the hereafter.
And so I asked him in return
What is it like when you feel loved?

He smiled and wiggled a little
And took a deeper breath.
He responded with a first word
And threw himself upon my bosom.

Hugged, he said, it feels like hugged
Or laughing and running wild.
Like being taken care of and getting better
When I am a very sick child.

That is heaven you feel
In lots of different ways.
For you to know it when you get there,
You must find it in all your days.

Alone

I am feeling so alone
Like that single cup upon the shelf.
It brings a tear upon my cheek;
Am I depressed or simply weak?
I shuffle around my home asking why?
My lonely dog breathes a heavy sigh
My laundry basket, I just don't care
Why am I breathing this familiar air?
I look around and see my chair
I remember the comfort given there.
I see the pot of fern I grow,
The books on the shelf,
Dear friends I have come to know.
The TV screen quiet now,
The kitchen table,
Two chairs in a row.
A warm crackling fire all aglow
With a kettle boiling ready to flow.
I wonder why I feel alone.
These friends of mine
Live in my home.

The Healing

She called me on the telephone.
Through the blustering wind outdoors
She told me her thunderous story,
And then...her rains began to pour.
As I listened to her voice
And the storm she pushed outside
With all her angst and force,
I knew what she was looking for.
A timeless place to find her fear
A name to call it, being very clear.
Putting all aside to be empty and calm
Listening alone might be the healing balm.
Wind and rain slowed down to start
A sunny period in time forgot.
Listening carefully and judging not
Is an act of love from my listening heart.

Both/And

I had a dream
That was disturbingly real.
A child of mine was lost
Gone forever – so surreal.

Hands wrenched together
Turning vivid blue.
Looking absolutely everywhere
Not finding you.

Sweating and chilling,
My body responds.
Blood vessels pulsating,
Uncontrollable fear abounds.

An ocean of hopelessness
Flows over me,
Drowning me in loneliness;
In all this world, where can you be?

I shudder into wakefulness
Realizing it was just horrible dreams.
Frightening feelings fighting reality,
I am falling apart at my seams.

The feelings linger on
And it feels somehow like
The both/and of life.
The mystery of reality and dreams of the night.
Like the differences within me of wrong and right?

How can I be giving and generous?
And still be stingy and bad?
How can I be sometimes happy?
And then overwhelmingly sad?

When I am worthy,
Medals and trophies proclaim my fame.
Then I fail in my sacred duties,
And I bring myself shame.

When will I accept what is life
Without making a choice?
When I rage like a lunatic
Or am grateful and rejoice.

Living is constantly dying
While dying is grasping to live;
Hoarding love and life,
Yet pouring out all I can give!

Sadness is comparing happiness;
Love can be heartbreaking pain and more.
Choice is other than and up against;
Everything *seems* to be either/or.

Within these realities of dream or life
Making living mysteriously grand.
Coming together in harmony
Everything contains both/and.

Gone Swimming

Once again I am thrilled
You have come!
I have waited the long night through.
I see you above
Walking toward me, stretching
Your beautiful body
Before entering into mine.
Our ritual of love
About to begin.
I feel you
Gracefully stimulating my stillness.
I feel your hands, arms, legs
Fluttering to and fro.
I am everywhere, here, there
Embracing you!
I desire to sooth you
Touch you, engage and excite you.
My gift to you:
Luxurious ripples of love.

What say you My Dearest?
Speak, for you are the one given
Voice!

I say I am here; I am here.
To paddle like a duck,
To swim like a swan,
To swish like a fish,
To float like a cloud,
To weightlessly dance,
Supported by you.

Your tender holding,
Your velvety enfolding
Flowing caress.
AND
I am grateful you have broken
From your voiceless silence.
For I have fallen deeply into
Our Maker's deep blue charm.
You, to which I daily succumb.

SEARCHING
IN MEMORIES

Birth

Silently I watch you.
My heart embraces you.
Softly I kiss you.
I long to know you forever.
I draw you nearer
That my single finger might stroke
Your perfect little face,
And that I might smell
Your perfect newborn smell.
New Child, endearing being,
Innocence divine.
You lie there
In peaceful, blissful slumber.
This is the hour
Your tiny fleeting smile
Lights up my universe.
God's appetite, for the deliciously beautiful
Expression of new life,
New love, new being.
Here we are womb into world
In the embrace of our belonging.

Son

When I lost that boy of mine
To another world outside of time,
An earthquake split my heart apart.
Cracking and splintering
The universe of my grounding.
Beliefs and knowledge I relied upon
Collapsed and crashed with frightening sound.
The blood in my veins pounded,
Wanting to erupt like hidden underground lakes,
Swishing in the deep parts of the earth,
Finding release in the depths of my wailing.
All alone
No projecting, no suspecting,
No rejecting.
A black hole of emptiness, forever apart.
The realms of the cosmos could not contain
This vibration of my broken heart.

The Pain of Love

Please – let me tell you
Of the silent, lonely
Pain of love
I experience
From time to time
For Ireland.

The beauty
And the sameness
Of the rain,
The land,
The people,
And their way.

The essence of life
Rising from the rhythm
Of monotonous days
With jobs to do,
That never end
And yet get finished.
And you hear them say,
It is done for the day.
And it is.

The good old sod,
Fields of grass,
And roads
And hedges
And flowers
And ferns
That require care,
Backbreaking care.

So the struggle goes on
To win the turf,
Grow the grass,
Feed the cows,
Clean the place,
Cut the hedges,
Do that job!
And then...
Stop for God!
At night
And Sundays too.
Old folks do it,
So others must too.

They wonder now and then
Just what it all means.
And what it is
They should dream of.
And sometimes without an answer
They simply respond
To the pain of love
And the rhythm of life.

And in that rhythm
A harmony is felt
As deep in their bones
As the dampness reaches.
And together they travel
To the heart.
And the pain of love
Resounds
And becomes anew
An integral part of Ireland.

And then
It is tomorrow again,
And they return to the land –
The struggles,
The defeats,
And the victories –
But most of all
The acceptance
Of broken things,
Never to be fixed,
That time will cover
With the land.

And their very own people,
Who get
A little broken too,
Piece by piece,
Not able to get fixed,
And sooner or later
Also
Get covered over with the land.

And though
The farm waits on,
And the turf
Still needs to be won,
The farmer and the land
Have finally become one.
And in the pain of love
His day is done.

It is now
Just a memory for me
Of when I felt whole,

And the beauty of Ireland
Filled my soul.
But before my days
Are finished and done,
I want to return there
To sit beside
The grave of my son,
For though we have been
So far apart,
The pain of love
Still fills my heart.

Irish Stew

It is the winter of my life.
I will go to hibernate with the bear.
Withdrawing into the cave of my soul,
I will find a comfortable place in there.

This I know for sure.
I will review my life and its recipe
Like the seasoned rugged fur of the bear
Or the rings inside the heaven-bound tree.

I will slowly burn memories
Like a heavy log upon a fire
Slowly diminishing into ash and soot.
Remembering the strong tree and the powerful root.

In my heart I will shine again
Like all the sunny days I basked in the light.
My wounded spirit will cry again
Like the many rainfalls
Of mistakes and shortsightedness.
I will gather these ingredients
And once again whip up
A fine Irish stew.
Blending in every thought, feeling,
Relationship and experience I ever knew.

The bear and I will feast upon
This delicious spicy Irish stew.
Shortcomings dark as night
Virtues bright as the sun.
My sacred meal will blend and savor
My beloved life into one!

P.S.
The bear and I will feast and dine
And dance till spring calls us forth,
For many a season might still renew,
A wintertime dance with a bear
And a brand new Irish stew.

SEARCHING
SIDEWAYS

Missed Opportunity

I missed the train,
Opportunity escaping down the track.
Absorption into a sponge of indecision;
Weighing pros and cons, calling them facts.

Feeling and knowing that it was only musing.
No longer finding it confusing.
Deciding to finally seize the day.
Too late; the train was on its way.

Lack of Communication and the Painting of the Floor

With great enthusiasm at ten years of age he volunteered to paint his bedroom floor.
I volunteered to tell him how to do the job.
He refused to listen and dashed off for paint and brush.
I found myself in a position of forcing instruction or allowing consequences to be the painting instructor.
I chose allowing consequences.

My husband, his father, closed his ears, or what felt like his heart,
To all of us around him who really mattered.
It was like he wanted to avoid communication,
Get away from anything that requires energy or thought.

"Do you need any help in there?" I asked my son, as I faced a closed bedroom door.
"No!" he replied, "I am smart and I know what I am doing – go away!"

Smart like your father, yes, he thinks he knows what he is doing, stashing away information like a squirrel hiding nuts for the winter.
Are you greedy or lazy, my thoughts back to my husband the avoider.
Situations are always arising. No responses, just looks that are demeaning, degrading.
I am not sure I can endure much longer.

So I tell him once again, "if we share, talk, listen to one another, there is so much potential for our relationship!
Please can you just give some thought to what I am saying?

We can share about anything, but oh the potential for our relationship."
The potential!
Avarice, greed, selfishness, and misery closed up like a locked dungeon door.
I give up – I don't want to be the one who judges, but I cannot stand it anymore!
No communication, no relationship. I quit!

Later on husband frowned and scorned at the idea of quitting,
And then followed up with the usual set-up he was so good at.
Hiding away, holding back, being suspicious, withdrawing till I could not take it anymore.
An explosion by me, a desperate attempt to wake him up
To life, to relationships I think he really did care about.
Then the nasty part of the set-up.
"What is *your* problem? Look how you are acting!" he would retort with a sarcasm and cynicism that would sting those who knew him.
He would later relate to a friend he drank with, only telling the explosion part.
Together they would laugh and sneer and justify his disdain.

I remember when my son painted the floor.
I saw him from the door in the farthest corner he had painted himself into.
"Mom" he said. "What can I do? Are there any ways I can get out of this?"
"Well" I said, "at least you are using the correct tool to get you where you want to be."
"What do you mean?" he asked, with genuine curiosity.
"Never mind" I said," let's talk about it until we find a way."

Poor ex-husband painted himself into a corner and stubbornly refused to see

That ordinary conversation is relationship reality! And the only way IN!

Missing the Mark

The rabbit saw the snake and froze.
Barely breathing, he glared with haunting eyes.
The snake hissed again,
Another hiss and then some sighs.

There she is again, the woman who annoys me.
I remember the day I heard what she said about me!
Like the snake hissing at the harmless bunny –
Not really biting, just hissing at me.

I don't forgive easily; I stash it away
Like the squirrel who stashes the nuts she finds.
I leave it there in the dirt of my mind.
Then when I need it, I dig it up again.

So there she was on this fine day,
Walking toward me with a smile and peaceful composure.
I dug up the nut in the murky memory of my mind,
And I hissed at her like a snake to dispose of her.

The potential for the present moment was lost,
The delicious nut the squirrel might have feasted on.
The possibilities I did not even bother to imagine;
What might have been was simply gone.

There is a part of me
That I usually never listen to
That knows it is my loss
Though I will not act on this with what I will do.

I will resist grieving the lost moment
I will tell my story and look for validation that I now miss,
For I am really more comfortable in anger
Where I allow myself to bury, to hide, and to hiss!

A Walk in the Snow

It snowed last night –
So beautiful a sight to behold,
Grounded in white and mirroring light.
She went for a walk in the snow.

She strolled and recalled what he said to her,
Anger within her beginning to stir.
She felt awkward, cold, out of step;
The developing storm made her eyes blur.

Why does he treat me like he does?
Why is he always so severe?
My boots are hurting; my face is cold.
Shivering now with judgment and fear.

Same old stuff all the time;
She will just drop him right out of her mind.
Deciding to not think of him anymore,
She noticed she was freezing to her very core.

Too much struggle; she decided to go back,
Ice cracking in her head.
Crunching snow, what a dread!
Homeward bound, she looked around.

Peculiar footprints in the snow –
She had been walking backward,
Away from the present moment.
No bright beauty or warm sunlight found.
Rather a stroll in her mind, not on the ground!

Peace

"Here son, are 50 plastic toy soldiers to play with"
Said the masterful father to his son,
Trying to pacify the approaching look on his young son's face.
Within minutes the boy returned
With the same approaching look.
"Where are your soldiers?" his father asked.
"I dug a hole and buried them in the ground"
The boy with subtle agitation replied.

"Why? Why, Son did you bury your toy soldiers
One and all?"
The boy replied quickly without much thought.
"Wars kill, soldiers kill, guns kill,
People die,
Again and again and again."
"Dad, can you reach up on my bedroom shelf?
I want to play my violin!"

Integrated Tragedy

The child came first from
A mother and a father
Like a plant from a seed
Or a river from a rain puddle.
A stone from hardened waste,
Which rotted from something before.
A tree becomes roots and limbs
To climb out of the large seed it was.
Everything the eye can see
Is linked to you and to me.
Even that which flows in us
Connects us.
Wherever we look inside, upward,
Downward, backward,
Or forward, someone,
Something is there.
We are connected, bonded, united:
Our common air!

The scariest fear of all,
The greatest frustration of all,
Is to feel alone, separated,
Isolated because of the untruth of it!
And even worse, even more frightful
Is to cause it ourselves while pointing at our kin
And refuse that vulnerable thread
That connects all
To the tapestry of the universe.
To deny our responsibility
For what we have done
To the vast network of "one"

And then to tell ourselves
Never will I say I am sorry;
Never will I admit how much
I am hurting myself
As well as all other.
Part of this great mystery...
This integrated tragedy!

SEARCHING
ENDED
~BEGINNING

Lying Down

When I finally lie down
To never rise again,
I will hear the wind crying out to me
Breathe deep, for our bond is profound.
The sun will say
Stand up, stand up and soak me in
For I have warmed you until I am familiar with
The very texture of your skin.
The stars will say
Look up at me, for I have influenced you
In ways you have neither discovered nor acknowledged.
I will miss your curious yet predictable
Gaze if you leave me now.
The moon will speak of her influence
And how she pulled the tides that created my moods
And because of this she knew me intimately
Even when I did not know myself.
The seeds I planted in the spring-times of my life
Always multiplying abundantly ever more seeds for the
future
Which I will not be here to plant again,
Or attend to, or harvest. These seeds whisper to me
That they will miss me
As will the very ground I planted them in!
That lush soil, which contains every living thing
That was here before in my garden of delight,
Bountiful in its decomposing nourishment.
This small piece of earth continues to wait
Patiently for all that is yet to come.
This soil still welcomes me to my garden
To remind me of how I touched her tenderly

As I dug and let her stony content
Free flow through my finger tips
Into my co-creating heart.

So now I ask
Will my children weep for me?
Some of them like a down pouring rain.
Others, ever so softly...mourning dew upon their cheeks?
Will they embrace the pristine love
That I bequeath them to swim in,
For now they must go deeper to recreate
Themselves in Motherless ways.

What then of the dear, dear friends
With whom I have shared myself
Vulnerable as a stained glass window
With secret dark shadows and bright colored revelations.
What of those I have influenced
Or healed or walked with
On a part of their journey, which was filled with pain and
suffering.
Will they cry because I am gone, or because now
They will journey with me only in memories?

As for me, I have lived a magnificent adventure!
Laughing and crying, suffering and surviving, dancing and
romancing
Pushed on by the gentle and sometimes fierce force of love
From family, friends and innocent bystanders.
Encouraged and supported by Mother Nature.
And it was all so awesome
So incredibly and unbelievably grand!
This life of mine.

I will go now to the great mystery of a God of love.
To whom I owe not only my remarkable life
But that one extraordinary singular grace...
Worth lying down to give my breath away!
That grace of simply consistently choosing to remember
And planning never ever to forget
For my next adventure.
A profound and unmistakable bond,
A union, an inseparable relationship
With a deliciously inconceivable God Who is Love!

About the Author

Growing up surrounded by the quiet Midwestern way of life, Jan Schomp began weaving the tapestry of her life, like that of fine Irish linen and lace. She worked hard to learn and practice her Catholic religion. For the most part though she turned to her Divine Connection. She did this for all the good reasons which good relationships can bring to a person.

Every time life began to fall apart for her and tug at the seams, she began to notice that the Divine was in the seams as well! Finally she came to the realization that her relationship with The Divine was absolutely everywhere in her life. This was the point when the design, the imprint, began to emerge as a love affair, upon the tapestry. She also came to the conclusion that love did not necessarily have anything to do with religion. Religion was not a bad thing, but for her it was not what it was about. Rather it was God loving her, no matter what!

Always interested in and the practice of writing poetry along the way, Jan began to reflect on and notice how this special relationship was manifested in every aspect of life and she started to write about it in her poetry. Thus "Searching" a collection of poems was born into being. These poems are of her heartfelt findings in the cloth of her own life and sometimes other's lives, seams and all!

Jan has worked as a Director of Pastoral Care for the Sisters of St. Joseph of Boston and as a Pastoral Associate in Florida. She is also a Spiritual Director. In her younger days she taught in several Catholic Schools.

For Jan though, her most important work was raising her 8 children. As she experienced the wonder of her children and their interactions with her and each other she felt such great love for each and every one of them and herself. Life became fulfilled. Finding the Divine in each one of them the fibers became strands of beautiful unique multicolored love. Even and especially sometimes while painful, it is love indeed that weaves the threads of all of life. Jan writes her poetry as a result of her constant searching for this ultimate reality, of love hidden in everyday life, even in the crevices of the seams.

CPSIA information can be obtained at www.ICGtesting.com
Printed in the USA
BVOW11s0928180915

418467BV00001B/2/P

9 781504 333832